Preparing to Celebrate with Children

Gerard Whitty, Jeanette Mercer and Elaine Wells

NOVALIS

Design: Eye-to-Eye Design, Toronto

Layout: Suzanne Latourelle

Illustrations: Eugene Kral

Series Editor: Bernadette Gasslein

© 1997, Novalis, Saint Paul University, Ottawa, Ontario, Canada

Business Office: Business Office: Novalis, 49 Front Street East, 2nd floor, Toronto, Ontario M5E 1B3

Novalis: ISBN-2-89088-798-7

Printed in Canada.

Canadian Cataloguing in Publication Data

Whitty, Gerard, 1945-
    Preparing to celebrate with children
(Preparing for liturgy)
Includes bibliographical references.
ISBN 2-89088-798-7

    1. Children in public worship—Catholic Church.
2. Children's liturgies. 3. Catholic Church—Liturgy.
I. Mercer, Jeanette II. Wells, Elaine III. Title.
IV. Series

BX 1970.2W55 1997   264'.02'0083   C97-900423-3

Contents

Introduction

Congratulations! By opening this book you are accepting to grapple with a vital issue: the full, active, conscious participation of our children in the Sunday assembly. It is a continuing concern of pastors, parents, musicians and children. Children are active subjects of liturgy, not passive recipients. When we reduce them to passivity we patronize and marginalize them; they become silent, voiceless, in our community.

We baptize our children and welcome them into the community as participants, not spectators. Our responsibility is to equip them to participate fruitfully and actively in the assembly's work. This responsibility begins for us when we baptize them, not when they come at seven or thirteen years of age to complete their initiation.

Recently, while preparing three children of catechetical age for initiation, an interesting conversation arose. During the catechesis on the eucharist, the children expressed grave concerns about going to mass every Sunday. It was just too boring for them. This was not the first time pastors, parents and educators have heard this. What is new, however, is that these children could express their views in a public forum. It is also new that someone listened to them and asked them what would improve the liturgy for them.

Many parents struggle with the issue of boredom every Sunday morning. Before Vatican II, the response to children's questions about the mass was that "It is a mystery; we cannot understand it." Today we know that the liturgy should not mystify anyone but should make sense to all, even children. Parents talk about the hassle getting children out to mass. One Sunday morning a ten-year-old said to his mother, "Can't we read the Bible at home today? No one really speaks to me in church." We wonder about the absence of children in our assemblies; about those who say they get little out of the liturgy; about their boredom.

How long can we turn a deaf ear to the experience of children or their parents?

In their formative years children absorb the world around them. Liturgy itself is formative and is a major influence in our lives. What we experience in liturgy gives us our sense of identity as a community. Children, as part of the assembly, absorb the world of the parish. They know when we include and welcome them. They also feel when we exclude and ignore them.

One of the important insights of the liturgical movement is that the liturgy is the work of the assembly. Since children are baptized into the assembly and are physically present on a Sunday morning, it follows that liturgy is their work, too. Liturgy is not exclusively an adult action. The church encourages us to move away from liturgies for exclusive age groups such as children, senior citizens or youth. "The Sunday assembly is inter-generational and one group benefits the other by their presence"(*Directory for Masses with Children*, [DMC], 16).

Getting to Know the Directory for Masses with Children

We present this book to you as a process. Groups or individuals, liturgy committees or parents, pastors or any interested persons may use it. The principal document to which we will refer is the *Directory for Masses with Children (DMC)*. It is a precious instrument with which we advise all to become acquainted. Please make sure that you have a pencil/pen and notebook handy, too. The book you're holding will help you reflect on your current practice, name it, uncover the reasons for your present action, and tease out what you now understand. At the end of various sections, you may take time to use the reflection questions *(in italics)* to help you write some of the thoughts that arise from your reading. Then in small groups, continue with discussion questions as indicated. They have been placed at the end of each chapter.

Ask some children you know (sons, daughters, grandchildren, nieces, etc.) to describe their experience of liturgy on Sunday morning. Really listen to them without judgment. What do you hear?

Reflect on last Sunday's liturgy. Remember all the ways children were participating as baptized members of the assembly. How were they respected?

AFTER REFLECTING, PLEASE GO TO DISCUSSION QUESTION BELOW.

In Summary

This book challenges the local assembly to give children a voice in their Sunday praise and worship. Hopefully, it will open avenues for children's full, active and conscious engagement in the symbols and rituals.

Discussion Question

Jamie feels that mass is boring. He has always gone with his family but now, at ten, he proposes that his family have their own prayer. He says, "At mass a bunch of people we don't know read from the Bible and talk about things I can't understand. The only thing we can't do here is have communion." He wants to stay home. How would you respond to him as his parent? as lector? as presider? as liturgy committee?

CHAPTER 1

Your Experience

The purpose of this chapter is to clarify your present practice of preparing children to participate fully, actively and consciously in your assembly. Throughout this booklet we will speak of the Sunday assembly as the norm. We are not referring to the school and any of its liturgies.

Naming Your Experience

Since the focus is the formative aspect of preparing to celebrate with children, it is crucial that you begin by looking at the formative aspect of your assembly. We invite you to start by looking at your present action and to ask some simple questions. How do you celebrate with children present among you on Sunday morning? What do you do and why do you do it that way?

An assembly's action indicates its belief about children and liturgy. Reflect on your present practice. From this will emerge the best way to introduce change or to build on what you do. Begin by naming your present practice in reflective process. As far as possible, probe what you have named to see why you chose these actions. We always have our reasons for doing what we do.

Find a space where each one of you can work in silence.

1.   *Standing within your assembly on a given Sunday, describe it as fully as possible.*

2.   *The ways we consult and include our children in the process of preparing liturgies are ...*

3.   *We foster the person and dignity of children as equal members of our assembly by ...*

4.   *Children are active in all our ministers, namely ....*

5.   *The formation they received was ....*

6. When children are present in our assembly we make the following adaptations to the liturgy ...

7. The adaptations are proposed and prepared by ....

8. We do not adapt the liturgy when children are present because ...

9. The music guidelines we follow for our choice of music when children are present in our assembly are ...

10. Our presider speaks to children directly during liturgy ...

11. Our assembly welcomes, supports and affirms families every Sunday by ...

12. The social influences and cultural backgrounds of our children that affect our preparation and celebration are ...

13. Sacraments in our assembly have nothing to do with age or school grade because ...

14. The initiation process in our parish is ...

15. When we celebrate initiation sacraments within the Sunday assembly, some parishioners go to another parish because ...

16. As I reread this, I feel and think ...

Other comments:

It is equally important to name the assumptions, reasoning, understandings and theories that each of you brings to the celebration. All of this affects your present practice.

Share your reflections with one other person. Listen without comment or judgment. Encourage participants to share with their partner only that with which they are comfortable. When all have shared, come together as a full group and allow some time to hear some of what was shared. Now shift the focus to a more critical stance. Invite participants to reflect on why we do what we do.

Looking at Tradition

Now that you have named the positive and negative realities of your situation, let's turn to the church's tradition. It is vital to bring your experience to the tradition, dialogue with the tradition, and allow it to challenge you while also challenging it.

Our rituals and documents embody the church's tradition. Using the *General Introduction to the Roman Missal*, we will explore the relationship between children and worship by looking at some general principles for preparing liturgy. (You will find a fuller treatment of general liturgical preparation in *Preparing and Evaluating Liturgy* in this series.) Then using the *DMC* we will look at the specifics of preparing liturgy at which children are present. Finally, we will apply the principles for liturgical preparation to the Sunday assembly to discover some of the possibilities open to you.

In Summary

1. Sometimes it helps to begin with your own experience of children's participation in your assembly.

2. It is important to go below the surface level of experience to name the assumptions that are at work, ask why we do what we do, and share our reflections with others.

CHAPTER 2

Spirituality and Children - Liturgical Foundations

In "The Parable of Childhood," Nathan Mitchell says that "children are precious because they are children, not because they are potential adults. They are a treasure not because they will one day grow up and be like us, but because they force us, like parables, to confront the unexpected, and to deal with a God who chooses to behave in an ungodlike manner" (*Celebrating with Children: Liturgy , Vol. 1, No. 3*).

Yet we still do not have an adequate theology of childhood. Children are so full of wonder, imagination and trust, just as we once were. They interact with the world with spontaneity, openness and awe. Ask any parent in your parish and they will share story after story of children's awareness of the sacred. Children have vivid religious imaginations.

Parents who observe children in their everyday lives witness their inborn understanding of ritual and symbol. Children bring their full lives to their every encounter. They live in their imaginations, enter into the world of symbols, are open to the future, and possess a liturgical sense of time and being. Children learn by imitation. An assembly that actively, fully, consciously and fruitfully worships week after week provides a natural example for children to imitate.

In my experience, the key ideas for a theology of childhood are ...

AFTER REFLECTING, PLEASE GO TO DISCUSSION QUESTION 1, P. 21.

Children and Jesus

Jesus was born and grew up in a family. By doing this, he has forever blessed childhood. Throughout his public ministry, he welcomed children. He took them in his arms, blessed them and held them up to his apostles as a model for discipleship. Their helplessness and the dependence constantly remind us of our grace filled relationship with God.

We do the opposite. We expect children to act grown up and to be like us, especially in church! One Sunday, a parishioner angrily claimed that children should act like adults when they are in church; they are so irreverent! Yet, Jesus encourages us to become like little children.

As I reflect on Jesus proposing a child as the model of discipleship I feel ...

AFTER REFLECTING, PLEASE GO TO DISCUSSION QUESTION 2, P. 21.

Children and the Church

Like its master, the church welcomes children. It accepts and initiates children as full members through the sacraments of initiation: baptism, confirmation and eucharist. Through the formative and transformative powers of liturgy and catechesis, the church shows its ongoing care and nurture for the children it initiates, not because they will be the future of the church, but because they are the church now.

What is important is baptism, not the age of the child. The Spirit of Jesus, poured out in baptism, makes these children priests, prophets and kings to serve our God. From this flows children's right and duty to participate in the liturgy. Without this, they could never take up their responsibilities to participate in the assembly.

To me, the implications of children's right and duty to participate in the liturgy are ...

AFTER REFLECTING, PLEASE GO TO DISCUSSION QUESTION 3, P. 21.

Children and the Local Assembly

Could it be true that if what we have said so far is right, the assembly needs conversion?

From the moment of baptism, children have a place in the assembly. They do not need permission to take their place or to participate. As a gathering of God's people, we are a credible sign of the kingdom only to the extent that we are a welcoming, inclusive community.

A credible assembly is open to everyone: adults and children; able bodied and disabled; domestic and homeless; poor and rich; strangers and neighbours; sinners and saints. The entire gathered assembly forms one, united community to hear God's word, to eat and drink as one body, and to be sent forth to mission as one body. When we send children to crying rooms or other places for homilies, we fragment the assembly. This action weakens its sign value.

The *DMC* intends neither to single out children nor to neglect adults. Each is vital to handing on our faith. They are vital for each other in human relationship. The interaction of adults and children in the local assembly is part of the process of socialization.

The role of children in our assembly is ...

AFTER REFLECTING, PLEASE GO TO DISCUSSION QUESTION 4, P. 21.

Children and Hospitality

Children have an acute sense of belonging, and know well when they are excluded. Hospitality is key to worship, not an option. Perhaps you can recall a time at school when a child sat alone at lunch time. When we are not welcomed or spoken to directly by people, we too feel isolated from those around us at the meal of the Lord's table.

Just look at how children celebrate birthdays. The doorbell rings and everyone runs to the door to welcome the new guest. They take her coat and receive her gift. There are stories to tell and games to play. All gather around the table together, sing the birthday song, and eat and drink together. Thanks is offered for the gifts and usually guests go home with a little gift as a remembrance of the party. Hospitality, real and authentic, is given freely and received humbly.

Welcoming is a verb, a word that denotes action. The assembly cannot delegate its responsibility for welcoming: merely saying words does not make us a welcoming community. It is much more than giving food and drink. It is an attitude that shows and shapes an appreciation for life. Hospitable people give the tools of worship to all who enter through the door of baptism, enabling them to interact according to their abilities. A hospitable community symbolizes the reign of God.

The local parish must be the living sign of Jesus, creating with our lives an atmosphere and environment for children and adults. We create and maintain the hospitable atmosphere by our presence, tone of voice, posture, facial expressions. The mutual, conscious acceptance of one another's presence opens us to full participation in the eucharist. When we adapt the liturgy to meet the needs of the children we are being hospitable to them.

As Catherine Dooley once said, "the purpose of adaptation is, on the one hand, to help the child better understand and participate, and on the other, to help the child realize that the Eucharist is a community celebration and the child is a member of that community. Liturgy for children is never to create a sense of separateness but always a sense of belonging to the entire ecclesial community."

The ministry in our parish consists of ...

We involve the children in our hospitality ministry by ...

AFTER REFLECTING, PLEASE GO TO DISCUSSION QUESTION 5, P. 22.

Children and Music

For each experience of humanity there is a song. Music is as much a part of human life as is food and drink. Our awareness of musical sound begins in the womb with the rhythm of the heart and the sound of the human voice. In our early years, music soothes and comforts, reassures and lulls. It is communication with the Creator.

Music plays a significant role in all human celebrations. It helps us mark the special occasions and milestones of our lives. What would a birthday party be without singing "Happy Birthday"? Who has not wondered at the ease with which children master tunes and lyrics? They have boundless enthusiasm for singing songs over and over.

As adults, we respond to music in the same way. It catches our attention, lifts our spirits, comforts our woes and enables us to participate in life's celebrations. Since music first touches the heart, it can speak to child and adult at the same time. Simple music, song and refrain, is prayerful for both children and adults. As in all things, children take cues from adults. When we enter into celebrations with joy and enthusiasm, so do they.

Guidelines exist for preparing music for the liturgical assembly. Music that reduces either children or adults to spectators is inappropriate. The guidelines call for quality music that is familiar, liturgically appropriate and pastorally sensitive. Liturgical judgment demands that "the nature of the liturgy itself will help determine what kind of music is called for, what parts are to be preferred for singing, and who is to sing them" (*Music in Catholic Worship*, 30).

Whether we are planning for adults, children or both, music intrinsic to the ritual is the most important (e.g. the acclamations in the eucharistic prayer). Music that is of good quality excludes the trite, the cheap, and most of what is on the hit parade. Pastorally sensitive music takes into account the actual circumstances of the assembly, enabling the assembly in its unique culture, place, and age, to express its faith. The cycles and seasons of the liturgical year provide occasions to use both traditional and contemporary song and music for the assembly.

The criteria our music ministry uses to make decisions about music when children are present in our assembly are...

Where does the emphasis fall? On the acclamations? The service music? The hymns?

The assembly always sings when ...

The assembly doesn't sing when ...

AFTER REFLECTING, PLEASE GO TO DISCUSSION QUESTION 6, P. 22.

Children and Family Life

Liturgists and planners need to recognize the relationship between family life and liturgical celebration. Family life is our first introduction to liturgical life in its domestic form. From the day they are born, children are prepared by their parents to participate in liturgy.

Families mark special occasions with joy, thanksgiving, praise and wonder, and respond with body gestures and actions like jumping, laughing, clapping and singing. When special occasions arise we decorate our homes appropriately for family celebrations that often involve storytelling and traditions. When encouraged and affirmed, children become willing participants in every aspect of these family celebrations.

Parents and children minister to one another in the home. Embraces or hugs ritualize the human experience of love and forgiveness every day. The pain and joy of everyday family life expresses the dying and rising of Jesus Christ. When we bring our human experience to our celebrations, the liturgy shapes, forms and transforms our attitudes and affections. We come to know who we are.

Our Sunday assembly affirms and supports parents and children by ...

Our liturgical celebrations connect with everyday family life by ...

AFTER REFLECTING, PLEASE GO TO DISCUSSION QUESTION 7, P. 22.

Children and Ministry

The Holy Spirit gifts us in the sacrament of baptism and pours out charisms on all the baptized. The local assembly is responsible for calling forth these gifts and charisms for the building up of the Body of Christ. We cannot assume that children must wait until adulthood to offer their gifts and have them recognized by the church.

In their homes, children greet their friends, visitors and guests. They tell all about their day and recount stories they have heard. Early on, children learn to help by setting the table for meals and bringing food to the table. With their parents, they plan and help organize celebrations, and clean up afterwards. It is not only natural, but necessary, to include children in the ways they can offer their gifts to the Sunday assembly.

When children want to help at home, we offer them formation, respect and support. When our children offer their gifts for ministry in the assembly, they require acceptance, respect, support and formation from the community.

Children serve in the following ministries: the local assembly, music ministry, lector, server, cross bearer, candle bearer, greeter, gift bearer and collector. Depending on local diocesan guidelines, they may also serve as eucharistic ministers. Their input is invaluable to those preparing the liturgy.

Ministry and children require careful preparation. The liturgical assembly, not the needs of any one child or adult "to do something," is the priority. Involvement in ministry does not mean giving each child a role just to have the appearance of everyone doing something.

The ministry of the assembly and full, active, fruitful participation of children is primary. Children and adults gather, listen to the word, give praise and thanks and are sent out on mission. So when children are gifted and called to undertake a particular ministry we must help them to understand they serve the people of God. If they are not gifted, called and formed for a particular ministry, it would be better to engage an adult minister than to have a child fulfill it poorly. Children do not have to do everything, but should be given ownership of their roles.

We recognize children and ministry, call them and form them by ...

The list of parish ministries open to children in our parish is ...

AFTER REFLECTING, PLEASE GO TO DISCUSSION QUESTION 8, P. 22.

Children and Symbols

Most of us grew up with the notion that symbols are things like bread and wine. Nathan Mitchell reminds us that symbols are verbs, actions we do, such as eating bread and drinking wine ("Symbols are Actions, not Objects," *Living Light,* vol. 13, # 11). They are personal and communal actions, not private and individual.

Symbols are worlds into which we enter. Only when we surrender to the power of ritual can we do this. Symbols involve the whole person—mind, body and spirit. Good human gestures and actions undergird every symbol. From this perspective, and recalling what we said earlier about how children relate to their surroundings, we can see that the world of the child is the world of symbol. Since the world of liturgy is the world of symbol, children are also at home in liturgy. Children can enlighten us on how to do our symbols with our whole person, sight, sound, smell, touch and taste.

Everything we do in liturgy involves our bodies. Washing in baptism, rubbing in anointing, eating real bread and drinking real wine in communion, singing, silence, listening, speaking, greeting and processing—all are strong, robust symbols that speak for themselves. Such ritual symbolic activity catches the imagination of and elicits a response from both adult and child.

The world of liturgy as a world of symbol leads me to ...

AFTER REFLECTING, PLEASE GO TO DISCUSSION QUESTION 9, P. 22.

Children and the Presider

The *DMC* makes the point that it is the presider's responsible making the celebration festive, familial and meditative (23). In his commentary on the *DMC*, Edward Matthews says "children need affectionate understanding, control and correction nicely blended so that, while youngsters may be producing a continuous hum of noise and movement, the presider is still in charge"(*Celebrating Mass with Children*, Collins: 1975).

Presiding is an art, not a science. There is no manual or recipe for presiders. Presiders are to create an atmosphere where the encounter with mystery is possible. This demands prayerfulness, silence and avoiding didactic teaching. It involves excluding foreign elements in the liturgy. So it may mean, "if the presider finds it difficult to adapt to the mentality of children sometimes inviting a lay person to preach the Word of God"(24).

> *Our presider includes children ...*

After reflecting, please go to discussion question 10, p. 22.

Children and Initiation

The Roman Catholic Church has a tradition of initiating children into the faith of the community. Currently we have two rites for the initiation of children: the adult rite adapted for children of catechetical age and the rite for baptizing infants.

The goal of baptism is life in the eucharistic community. When an assembly initiates a child into its faith, it assumes an awesome responsibility. Life in the eucharistic community begins the day of baptism, not years down the road, and so does the assembly's responsibility. We are to welcome, support and empower children to deepen their faith as they grow and mature. Every Sunday, the gathering of the people of God forms the faith of our children. We are to enable children to take their place in this eucharistic assembly.

> *Reflect on how you form children to take their place in the assembly ...*

After reflecting, please go to discussion question 11, p. 23.

In Summary

1. Jesus seriously proposed children as a model of discipleship; the church welcomes and baptizes them.

2. The child rightly belongs to the assembly.

3. It is the responsibility of the aseembly, in particular, the presider, music director and parents, to give children the tools to worship and minister fully, actively and consciously.

Discussion Questions

1. Kate wants her four-year-old son to see going to mass as an extension of what her family do already. Step into her shoes and speak as her son's advocate.

2. People gather at the entrance of the church to begin mass. William is happy to be there greeting his friends. An elderly parishioner comes up behind William, pulls off William's baseball cap and puts it in his hand, mumbling about "respect." William is confused and taken off guard. He asks his mother if he has done something wrong. What was William doing? What was the elderly parishioner doing? How would you propose to have the two dialogue? As his mother, what would you say to him?

3. Meghan cannot see over the people in front of her. When the liturgy is long she becomes frustrated and restless. She does not want to leave her dad to go out with the other children for the word. Her dad doesn't want to sit any closer to the front because Meghan is restless and might disturb other parishioners. Can Meghan enter into the liturgy? Is Meghan "the church now"?

4. A young couple comes to mass with their infant. She is a little fussy and begins to cry during the homily. One of the ushers kindly suggests that the crying room is available near the front of the church. They decline the offer but leave after the homily. What is important to the assembly?

5. Eight-year old Rachel heard about ministry sign-up in her parish. She had just completed full initiation and was ready to take up her role in the assembly. With her parents' help, she signed up for the ministry of hospitality, making a commitment for one year. Kate's name was entered on the list, but no one ever called her. After months of expectation, she was disillusioned about ministry. Discuss what you would do upon hearing of this situation.

6. The liturgy committee is preparing for Lent. It is suggested that, for the penitential rite, we sing the Kyrie. Some parishioners think it will set the tone for the season. The assembly also includes many children with no experience of the pre-Vatican II liturgy. How is a decision made for the whole assembly?

7. Seven-year-old Alex learned to drink from a cup long, long ago. However, when he receives from the cup at communion, the minister holds the cup for him, pouring into his mouth. He feels intimidated and out of place. At what age does the dignity of the person become important?

8. Your six-year-old granddaughter has seen you as a eucharistic minister as long as she can remember. She has always imitated your every action at home and now she wants to follow your lead by doing ministry. What would you say to her about ministry? How could you see her ministering in the Sunday assembly?

9. For the baptism, lots of water was poured so that the sound of splashing could be heard all over the church. Then the presider dipped his hands into the chrism and began to anoint the baby's head, rubbing the oil slowly and with care. From the assembly a small but loud voice could be heard: "Look, mommy, he's shampooing the baby's hair!" Discuss how symbols, without explanation, can capture the same meaning for all.

10. We have all had occasion to preside over functions: parties, dinners, meetings, etc. Pick one occasion when you presided and name your primary function.

11. A single mother of three requests baptism for her newborn. She wants the baby baptized but has no relationship with any community. She does not believe going to church is necessary but does go for Christmas, Easter, weddings and other special occasions. She has already made the baptismal promise to raise her other two children in the practice of the faith, but has not followed through. Can children be formed in the faith of the eucharistic community if they are not present? How can the assembly fulfil its role in the absence of some of its members?

CHAPTER 3

General Principles for Preparing Liturgy

In this chapter we will explore some general principles for preparing liturgical celebrations. Since another booklet in the series deals with this, we will emphasize only those that speak to celebrating with children.

Let's look at seven principles that directly affect children in the assembly.

1. Liturgy is the Work of the Entire Assembly

This simple statement captures the paradigm shift in our understanding of liturgy. Not too long ago we would have agreed that liturgy is the work of the ordained priest. The gathered assembly gives praise and thanksgiving to God. The corollary to this insight is that liturgy belongs to all. It is the work of the entire gathered people in a given time; no one does liturgy for us. Therefore, the primary minister is the assembly.

Everyone must be able to own what we do in liturgy. When the Sunday liturgy is owned by one person or group, it becomes divisive and reduces the assembly to the role of spectator. All own baptism, eucharist, and ordination but can all own Scout's Day, or installations of the Catholic Women's League, the Knights of Columbus or the Holy Name Society?

For a spirituality grounded in liturgy, the liturgy must belong to the assembly, a unified, inclusive assembly. If we initiate our children and they are present in the assembly, then the liturgy belongs as much to them as to the adults who are present.

> *Some actions in our liturgical assembly that I do not own are*
> ...
>
> *Are there any actions in our liturgical assembly that exclude children? women? men? Name these actions.*

AFTER REFLECTING, PLEASE GO TO DISCUSSION QUESTION 1, P. 30.

2. The Work of the Assembly is the Praise and Glory of God

We do not need to reinvent liturgy every time we come together. We already have a tradition handed down from our Jewish and Christian ancestors. From beginning to end liturgy is an act of praise and thanksgiving. As an example, let's look at the Sunday eucharist.

That we gather is an act of praise, a wonderful deed of God's Spirit that allows us to come together. The word of God proclaimed in the midst of the assembly is taken from the account of God's mighty deeds for our salvation. It is proclaimed with praise and thanks for all God is doing in our lives. The eucharist is a meal, the sharing of bread and wine. Around the table of Christ's body and blood we give thanks for the great deed of our salvation, the dying and rising of Jesus Christ. Then we are sent forth to proclaim the good news with lives of love and justice.

> *Reflect on your response to the presider who begins the liturgy "The theme of our Mass today is ..."*

AFTER REFLECTING, PLEASE GO TO DISCUSSION QUESTION 2, P. 30.

3. Liturgy Celebrates the Paschal Mystery of Jesus Christ

One of the greatest gifts of the Second Vatican Council was a reclaiming of the paschal mystery, the dying and rising of Jesus Christ, as the root metaphor of Christian life. Every sacrament celebrates the paschal mystery. Sacraments are not meant to be celebrations of events in our life cycle. One day at a workshop, a participant said to me, "Surely there is more to the sacraments than the paschal mystery."

Baptism is the celebration, not of the birth of a child, but of rebirth in the fontal waters. The baptismal waters symbolize the dying and rising of Christ. In baptism we are plunged into the paschal mystery and the life of Christ. The paschal mystery is the pattern of all Christian discipleship: no one stands outside it. Our challenge today is to put the mystery of Christ's death and resurrection at the heart of our spiritual and liturgical life.

The ways I live out and enflesh the paschal mystery in my everyday life are ...

Children live out the dying and rising of Jesus Christ by ...

AFTER REFLECTING, PLEASE GO TO DISCUSSION QUESTION 3, P. 30.

4. Liturgy is Ritual Symbolic Activity

Neither ritual nor symbol receive good press in the modern world. People in our culture tend to equate ritual with boring activity and symbols with what is unreal. (We say "It's only a symbol.") Since the Sunday liturgy is of the order of ritual and symbol, it may not be seen as having any real value in our lives. Yet our everyday lives from dawn to dusk are of the order of ritual and symbol: waking, showering, dressing, eating and drinking, working, recreation and the things of family life.

Key to understanding symbols is seeing them as actions, not things. Symbols are verbs; they denote doing something. Symbols of married love are hugging, kissing and a lifetime of loving actions, not a ring. A symbol of the eucharist that pushes us out into the world to feed and nurture neighbour is not bread and wine, but eating and drinking. The act of anointing oil consecrated by the bishop, not the oil itself, is the symbol for the anointing of the sick. Bathing and washing in water is the symbol of baptism, not water.

To understand the world of robust ritual symbolic activity, pay attention to the foundations on which they are built: good human gestures.

The root of some of our problems in ritual symbolic activity is the lack of attention we pay to good human gestures. We trickle water from a shell instead of baptizing by immersion. We daub thumb in cotton wool and oil to anoint the sick instead of rubbing with lots of oil. We eat wafers made of flour and water instead of eating real bread and drinking real wine for Eucharist. When it becomes necessary to explain what our symbols mean, we leave ourselves open to the criticism that they are minimalist, routine, boring and unreal.

One of the ways to perceive ritual is to view it as doing its work over time rather than instantly. Rituals and symbols only work if we allow ourselves to surrender to them. Ritual has a both a formal and conventional dimension.

When we enter ritual it accomplishes what it sets out to do. When I walk up to you, shake your hand and say "Hello," we enter a ritual that is formal and conventional. We will negotiate that relationship if we accept the restraints of the ritual. It will not work if we ignore the restraints of convention and formality. If we accept the ritual of introduction, we, as two strangers, enter a relationship.

The ritual symbolic act we call liturgy not only says something about our relationship with God, but actually brings about that relationship. This relationship says something about our connection to self, others and the world we inhabit. Ritual does not celebrate my personal private world of feelings, thoughts or faith. It is a social, communal action that shapes and patterns our affections, attitudes and beliefs. This work doesn't happen in an instant but through a lifetime of lived service in the world. The test of religious ritual is not in the ritual itself but in a life lived in fidelity to the gospel and in service to the world. For further reading in this area, you may want to consult an article by Mark Searle, "The Uses of Liturgical Language," *Liturgy* 4, (1984), 15-19.

For me, the implications of this insight for preparing liturgy are ...

AFTER REFLECTING, PLEASE GO TO DISCUSSION QUESTION 4, P. 31.

5. Liturgy Demands the Full, Active and Conscious Participation of All

Thirty years after the Second Vatican Council we can see how this principle is both necessary and difficult to implement on the local level. The only way we can say that the liturgy is the work of the entire people in the community is if everyone in the assembly participates and is seen to participate.

Liturgy cannot have spectators. No person or groups of people can own the liturgy or do it for us. We, as assembly, are the subject of the liturgy; the ritual is our communal action. This is one of the reasons we say that the primary minister of the liturgy is the assembly. Praise and thanks is our communal response to the dying and rising of Jesus Christ.

We make adaptations in the liturgy to empower and enable the assembly to participate fully, actively and fruitfully in the ritual action. Participation involves our whole person: bodies, emotions, thoughts, and spirits. Liturgy is not a purely intellectual activity.

> *Our assembly encourages the active participation of men, women and children in the liturgy by ...*

PLEASE GO TO DISCUSSION QUESTION 5, P. 31.

6. Liturgy Unfolds the Whole Mystery of Christ Over Time

The rhythms of the liturgical year are important for a liturgical spirituality. The principle of the liturgical year is that the whole mystery of Christ unfolds over time. It takes time to tell and to savour the story of the virgin birth of Jesus, his life and teaching, his death and resurrection, and the virgin birth of the church at Pentecost. We celebrate the saints and Mary to remind us that the paschal mystery takes as many forms as there are people. The saints remind us also that heaven is attainable for all of us.

The liturgical year offers three challenges to the local assembly. First, when people worship only periodically, not moving through the liturgical year, they come to know only bits and pieces of the whole story of Christ. For example, if many in the assembly at Midnight Mass are there for the first time since last year, hospitality would demand that those who prepare the liturgy take this into account.

Second, those who plan and prepare liturgy need to challenge the assembly to keep the liturgical seasons together in balance and focus. (Lent-Easter is one season, not two; Advent-Christmas is also one season.) Sometimes we put all our energy into Lent and leave Easter to fizzle out, even though Easter is the climax of the whole liturgical year.

The third challenge for those who prepare liturgy is to ensure that the first Sunday of each season marks a clear beginning. Often we drift from one season to another, leaving most people unaware of the transition.

> *As I reflect about time and the seasons of my life what strikes me is ...*

AFTER REFLECTING, PLEASE GO TO DISCUSSION QUESTION 6 ON P. 31.

7. The Proclamation of the Word is Essential and Central to the Celebration of Liturgy

The eucharistic story of the disciples on the road to Emmaus expresses the importance of the scriptures for the spirituality of the liturgy. It was after they shared their fears and hopes and before the breaking of the bread that Jesus opened the scriptures to them, beginning with Moses and the prophets, and interpreting the things in all the scriptures referring to himself.

Jean Leclerq tells us that Jesus is the only book worth reading. Not only is he the book, he also reads himself. Jesus is present in the word proclaimed to the assembly. Today, with the advent of television, people are more visual than aural. This presents a challenge because, for ritual and liturgy, storytelling is essential. Readers must be very good storytellers to capture and hold the attention and imagination of the assembly.

Some assemblies are experimenting with creative ways to tell the scripture story, such as mime, drama and liturgy of the word with children. In liturgy of the word with children, it is important to focus on the word. Children go forth to hear the same proclamation the adults are hearing. Reading from any other source is inappropriate. The liturgy of the word with children is liturgy, not baby sitting or nursery. The length of proclamations may be adapted to the age and circumstances of the children, but the readings from the lectionary must be used.

Jot down your fears and hopes and then re-read the story of the two disciples on the road to Emmaus ...

AFTER REFLECTING, PLEASE GO TO DISCUSSION QUESTION 7 ON P. 31.

In Summary

1. There are many principles for preparing liturgy. Here we have named what we believe are the seven key principles to keep in mind when preparing liturgies with children present in the assembly.

Discussion Questions

1. An eighteen-month-old listens to the Easter Alleluias. All are standing for the gospel but she sits behind her parents singing loudly, "La, la, la, la." Discuss how an eighteen-month-old can enter into and own the liturgy.

2. Susan feels it is important that her three children are formed by the liturgy. The liturgy committee has decided to implement some principles of the *DMC* at one mass a month. Susan says to them, "No, my children need a place *every* Sunday." If children are called to be among us, how do we make allowances for their acts of praise and thanksgiving?

3. Fifteen-year-old Chad is preparing to celebrate confirmation this Easter. He and his father talk to the initiation team member, explaining why he wasn't confirmed last year. Chad was doing drugs and had attempted suicide. His parents' divorce became final around the same time. They have undergone counselling and are attempting, with much pain and difficulty, to put life back on track. As the initiation team member, what would you say to this family about the paschal mystery of Jesus Christ?

4. "I do not get anything out of ritual so I don't go to mass any more." Reflect on this from your point of view as an adult and from the child's viewpoint.

5. The choir prepares to sing its best for the Easter Sunday morning liturgy. If the choir director does not allow four-part harmony, some of the members are likely to leave. Discuss in light of full, active, conscious participation.

6. Discuss how you might close Ordinary Time and open the season of Advent in your parish. How could children be involved? How could adults participate?

7. The children were drawing what they heard in the gospel. A five-year-old boy drew boxes with bows. When he shared what he heard in the reading he spoke of "the presents of God." God speaks to each of us in God's word. Children have a right to hear the word of God as it is written. Discuss.

CHAPTER 4

Through the Lens of the *Directory for Masses with Children*

The reform initiated by the Second Vatican Council is over. The renewal is just beginning. Ten years after the close of the council, Rome gave us a document that addresses the full, active and conscious participation of children in worship. The *DMC* provides clear guidelines to light our way in preparing liturgies for adults with children present. In this chapter we will outline some of the principles of this document.

1. If we allow any liturgy to remain incomprehensible to children, we inflict harm on their faith and their spiritual life. The goal of ritual and liturgy is not to mystify. Liturgy makes sense. Those who prepare the liturgy must adapt symbols to the capacity of children to understand. Liturgists prepare liturgy according to the time, age, needs and circumstances of the participants. Children have different needs than adults. To meet the needs of children we can retain, shorten, omit certain texts or make a better selection. This we can do without throwing everything out and creating a new rite.

2. Human gestures and actions are essential to good liturgy. Greeting, listening, friendship and sharing a meal encode human values. In liturgy we stretch these gestures to include Christian values. The best preparation for liturgical prayer is our family life where values are taught and caught in the home. Presiders and planners need to assume the responsibility to make celebrations festive and reflective without using childish speech or being didactic.

3. Speak directly to children whether you are presider or parishioner. It is amazing how often we ignore children in our midst. We often speak to the parent and ignore the child. The *DMC* encourages us to speak directly to children in our introductory comments, our homilies and before the dismissal.

4. Movement, singing, gestures, visuals and silence are crucial. Children love the movement of processions. There are several processions in the liturgy where children might be invited to participate. The human voice is the instrument for liturgy and children love to use theirs in song. They also love to play musical instruments.

   If children and adults experience liturgy as dry and intellectual, it may be that we do not pay enough attention to visuals like candles, vestments and colours. It also may be that we fail to provide opportunities for children to reflect in silence.

5. Never omit or paraphrase scripture readings, or substitute readings from secular, popular sources for them. We may omit the first and second readings but the gospel is never to be omitted. We may omit a line or choose a more appropriate reading, always with quality, not quantity, as the criterion. Christ is present and speaks to all, adults and children, in the word proclaimed. Our role is to help children make a living response to the gospel; this is possible if we help children make the word their own.

6. Open ministry to children without destroying the ministries of others in the assembly, especially the ministries of adults. By inviting families to prepare the gifts and the altar, to be part of the ministry of music, proclaim the word when they are prepared and formed, join the procession with cross and candles, we are intensifying their participation. The challenge for us is to do it without destroying their awareness of their primary ministry as an assembly.

7. The seasons of the liturgical year unfold and tell the whole story of Christ over time. Today we are faced with an interesting phenomenon, that is, people who know bits and pieces of the story. Those who go yearly to Midnight Mass know the birth story well, but may not know the resurrection story. Those who go to the Good Friday service know the passion story, but may not know the birth story.

No one season can tell the whole story effectively. When children and adults gather, it is important to mark the seasons so that all experience movement through the liturgical seasons. Liturgy planners and presiders do this by changing liturgical colours intentionally, making a definite shift in music and song, doing strong ritual gestures and symbols, changing the liturgical space, art and environment. All of this enables us to enter into the season and respect its purpose.

8. Know the structure and meaning of the ritual. Entrance rites gather people and prepare them to hear the word of God. The essential rites are the greeting and the opening prayer. The other rites are secondary. In the liturgy of the word, God speaks to us. The Word of God, Jesus, for whom we give praise and thanks, speaks. In a meal, the liturgy of the eucharist recalls the death and resurrection of Jesus for whom we give praise and thanks. Jesus is the bread of life, food and drink for God's people. The dismissal rite sends us out into the world to continue Christ's mission. The *DMC* encourages us to adapt, yet remain faithful to the integral structure of the eucharist.

The *DMC* is our guide for celebrating with adults when children are present in the assembly. It is intended for liturgies with preadolescent children. The norm is not children's masses as we knew them in the past, but the eucharist with adults in which children participate. The normative celebration is the Sunday assembly, not the school mass.

From my reading of the Directory, *I would add ...*

In Summary

1. The *DMC* expresses our rich tradition. This chapter invites you to a conversation between the experience you worked on in chapter 1, and the tradition as expressed in the *DMC*.

Discussion Question

Now it is time now to stop and reread the experiences you got in touch with at the beginning of this booklet. When your experience has settled in your consciousness, begin a conversation with the tradition of the church as reflected in the documents. The following may help you.

> *What affirmed my experience was ...*
> *What challenged my experience was ...*
> *I agree with the tradition when it says ...*
> *My problems with the tradition are ...*
> *I am puzzled by ...*
> *I am intrigued by ...*
> *I need to pursue the following points or areas ...*

CHAPTER 5

Applying the Principles

Now it is time to return to action. In this chapter we will take a look at the implications for the Sunday assembly in a given parish of all the work we have done in this book.

The *DMC* was published in 1973. Implementation has been slow and uneven. The document maintains that we do not need to create a new rite when children are in our assembly. We can adapt while respecting the structure of the present rite. How do we accomplish this?

The Gathering Rite

Worship space and environment need preparation before the liturgy begins. The liturgy committee initiates the process of inviting and forming families to do this ministry. There are plates and cups, bread and wine, purificators and bowls, cross and candles, vestments and sacramentaries, lectionaries and microphones, hymnals and bulletins to be put in place. Families doing this ministry gain precious, hands-on learning experience.

This experience can also challenge the liturgy committee to look at the quality of some of the objects the community is using for eucharist. Do these really look like cups and plates? Are these really towels? Is this processional cross too heavy for children to carry? Can children lift these processional candles? Does this look, feel, taste like real bread?

The *General Instruction on the Roman Missal* states that the gathering rites have a twofold purpose: they form us into a community; they prepare us to hear the word of God. The usual format for the gathering rites on Sunday is: procession of ministers, hymn, sign of the cross and greeting, introductory words, penitential rite, Lord have mercy, Glory to God, and opening prayer. This is a long and verbal gathering rite, especially if the people are already in their places! The main thing is to ask, "Does it accomplish the stated purpose?"

This is especially long for children. The *DMC* acknowledges this and gives us some recommendations. It recommends that we retain the trinitarian blessing, the greeting and the opening prayer. Some of these rites can be omitted or shortened. (For more on this, see *Preparing to Preside* in this series.) It is important that the presider and the adults pay attention to the children in our midst and speak to them directly.

Children love processions. Invite children and adults to join the procession with the other ministers. Remember that we do not ask children to do what we as adults will not do. When both children and adults process no one is singled out or on display.

- The procession should allow children to be children: running, walking, swinging banners, singing the opening antiphon, playing musical instruments. Have joyful processions!

- A family could carry the cross and candles.

- Invite a child to carry the lectionary.

- As the assembly moves through the seasons, make sure the children have what is necessary to celebrate. At Easter ensure that people have candles, on Passion Sunday that they have palm, on Ash Wednesday that they receive ashes. Sometimes it is easy to forget children.

- The music ministry accompanies the procession through the worship space. This kind of procession challenges the music ministry to find music and song in which all can participate without books and sheets.

When the procession ends, the presider invites people to silence and prayer. Silence is important after this much movement. Children can enter into silence. The presider gathers the people's prayer together in the opening prayer. Here again, the *DMC* allows us to adapt. We can shorten the prayer by omitting difficult phrases.

> *Look at the gathering rite in your parish on a given Sunday. Name some adaptations you would like to see ...*
>
> AFTER REFLECTING, PLEASE GO TO DISCUSSION QUESTION 1, P. 44.

Liturgy of the Word

The gathering rites prepare us to hear the word of God. The liturgy of the word follows this pattern:

First Reading	Silence
Silence	Alleluia Verse
Psalm	Gospel and Homily
Second Reading	Creed and Intercessions

When children are in the assembly on Sunday, the liturgy committee needs to carefully examine the readings. The quality of the readings, not the quantity, is the norm. Since the proclamation calls for a response from the assembly, some of whom are children, then the readings must be able to reach the hearts of the children. Children cannot respond if the language is beyond their grasp. Years of listening to readings not understood leaves the impression that the word has no significance for their lives.

The *DMC* states that although the gospel is never omitted, the first and/or second reading may be omitted. Here are some questions to ponder as a committee:

> *Are the readings too long? ...*
> *Are they comprehensible to children? ...*
> *Would it help the children make the word their own if the readings were shortened? ...*
> *How will the adults respond to such a decision? ...*

The dignity of the word demands that a trained lector from the word ministry do the proclamation. The guiding rule is to have good proclamation. Children should not be expected to do a ministry at the risk of doing it poorly just so they are present in the ministry.

Your liturgy committee faces two concerns or challenges with the liturgy of the word when children are present.

First, do we dismiss our children?

Some communities dismiss children rather than change the readings when they are present. They have a separate room in which, respecting their age and level of growth, a leader will continue the liturgy of the word. Sending the children out has nothing to do with grades or classes. Neither does it have to do with baby sitting or enabling the adults to hear the proclamation church in peace and quiet. Nor is it a time to entertain children with "kiddy lit," or children's stories. This is the liturgy of the word, and the book from which our stories come is the lectionary.

Fragmenting the Assembly?

But when we send the children to a separate room we fragment the assembly we have just gathered! An alternative is to keep the assembly together and proclaim the word to the gathered assembly by adapting the liturgy to the needs of the adults and children in the assembly.

> *Why would we dismiss children from something in which they can participate and bring them back at a time when they can only participate visually?*

If there are children of catechetical age in the adapted catechumenate, they are dismissed after the gospel. We might consider waiting until after the gospel to dismiss all the children who are baptized, but who have not been confirmed or participated fully at the table of the eucharist. It is inhospitable to make these children stand and only watch people eat and drink the body and blood of Christ. If, at this stage in their lives, children stay in the assembly, they become spectators rather than participants. The assembly may not want to give this message to their children, a message family and assembly alike will have to change later.

Preaching and Children

The second concern the liturgy committee might have to address is the homily. Preaching to include children in the assembly demands certain gifts that some presiders do not have. Furthermore, if there is any hope of including children, a presider needs to have some relationship with them. Classroom techniques, childish talk, and speaking in patronizing ways have no place in the homily.

The *DMC* states that if a presider is uncomfortable speaking to children, he may invite a qualified lay person to give the homily. But the *DMC* encourages whoever gives the homily to include children and speak directly to them, not through their parents or puppets or other gimmicks.

The creed and intercessions conclude the liturgy of the word. The Apostles' Creed is suggested in the sacramentary, but sometimes the assembly could use the baptismal creed with its triple questions. There are also musical settings of the creed in *Catholic Book of Worship III.*

The intercessions are the community's petitions. They are not canned prayers to be read out of a book. The liturgy committee needs to craft these prayers in such a way that the assembly can see itself in them. It is a time in the liturgy when the community voices its concrete and ordinary day-to-day concerns overcoming the split between life and faith. Maybe the assembly could experiment with praying the intercessions spontaneously or with song and gesture.

Some options I would like to work with in our parish are ...

AFTER REFLECTING, PLEASE GO TO DISCUSSION QUESTION 2, P. 44.

The Liturgy of the Eucharist

The liturgy of the eucharist follows the four-fold action of Jesus at table on the night before he died. The scripture tells us that he took bread and wine, said the blessing (not over the bread and wine but blessed God), broke bread and poured wine, and gave it to his apostles. Let's explore each of these actions in the context of children in the eucharist.

Take

Taking bread and wine corresponds to preparing the altar and gifts for eucharist. Most parishes have a ministry of bringing forward the bread and wine to the altar. We can expand this ministry to include families who would come forth from the assembly and prepare the table. They could light the candles, place them on the altar, bring the sacramentary, place it on the altar, and provide the towel and bowl for the washing of hands.

While one family prepares the table, another family could prepare the gifts for the procession to the altar. A mistake some make here is having children bring up in the procession signs of their life and work such as basketballs, books or teddy bears. All we must bring forth is enough bread and wine for this assembly in this eucharist. The procession affords another opportunity for festive movement with lots of music and instruments. As we have said, children love processions! A deeper spiritual significance of this ritual action is to prepare to offer our lives to God.

Bless

Jesus, after taking bread and wine, praised and blessed God. The gathered church now does what Jesus did. Our prayer of blessing, thanksgiving, and praise to God is the eucharistic prayer. During this prayer we ask God to send the Holy Spirit to change not only the bread and wine but also us, personally and communally. We recall the dying and rising of Jesus Christ and unite our dying and rising with his.

Three eucharistic prayers are written especially for the times when adults and children are present together in the assembly. The prayers are simple, yet not simplistic; their acclamations provide more opportunities for children and adults to participate, and give more opportunity to balance sung and spoken word. The *DMC* suggests that, before the preface, the presider pause and invite the assembly, children and adults to name that for which they are grateful. It is also important to ensure that children pray the other eucharistic prayers proclaimed in the assembly. When they are used, pay attention that children too can sing the music of the acclamations.

Break

Jesus' third action was the breaking of the bread. During this time, bread is broken and wine is poured. We get ready to receive his body and blood. For centuries this gesture was so important that the name for the whole action of the eucharist was called "the breaking of the bread."

Again we return to the significance of human gestures so important to our liturgy. Taking a loaf of bread and breaking it speaks worlds to the assembly. The more attention we pay to the human gestures in this ritual, the easier it is to grasp the deep spiritual significance of this rite. For both children and adults, the bread must taste, smell and look like real bread and be large enough to be broken into smaller pieces. The action speaks of our solidarity and unity as an assembly, while also rousing our diversity and claiming the reconciliation won for us by Jesus.

Music and song accompany the gesture and action during the breaking of bread. The challenge to the music ministry is to choose music that does not exclude children but includes all. When this action concludes, eucharistic ministers come forward to take the prepared plates and cups to communion stations. A family could bring forward any extra plates, cups and purificators that are needed for communion at this time.

Eat and Drink

Jesus' fourth action was to distribute the blessed bread and cup. This is the ritual climax of the whole eucharist, becoming what we eat, the body and blood of Christ. Another procession calls for festive, joyful movement with music and song. Again, the music ministry must lead the assembly with music that includes children.

Children are not to be excluded automatically from the cup. They are to be treated with the dignity that their baptism affords them. Children who are confirmed can be eucharistic ministers unless diocesan policy forbids them from doing so.

> *The positive side of these adaptations ...*
> *My difficulty with these suggestions is ...*
>
> AFTER REFLECTING, PLEASE GO TO DISCUSSION QUESTION 3, P. 44.

The Rite of Sending Forth

Following communion we need time for shared silence, an action that all do together. It should not be broken, even visually, by anyone preparing for the next action. We are wrong to assume that children cannot enter silence and prayer.

If children were dismissed to a separate place to continue to reflect on the word, they return now for the final blessing. The *DMC* recommends that the presider recall the homily in a few words. The assembly is blessed and sent forth to live lives of love and justice.

The rite of sending forth is so short that we could miss it completely and lose its spiritual meaning: "As long as you did it to the least, you did it to me (Matthew 25: 40)."

The gathering could continue over coffee, juice and donuts, extending the hospitality begun at the gathering rite. This is another opportunity to invite children and families to minister by setting up the space, getting the refreshments, and hosting the gathering. Before everyone departs, another ministry involving children and adults is available. The worship space needs some last minute care: there are cups and plates to clean and wash, hymnals to return to their places.

> *For me the sending forth of our assembly each Sunday means ...*
>
> AFTER REFLECTING, PLEASE GO TO DISCUSSION QUESTION 4, P. 44.

In Summary

1. This chapter invites and challenges.

2. It invites the assembly to work with the guidelines in the *DMC*, not as the final word, but as a catalyst for beginning.

3. It invites the assembly to continue to struggle with the vision in the *DMC*.

Discussion Questions

1. The assembly welcomes families with children for baptism at the entrance to the church. What similarities are there in the way we enter the church through the gathering each Sunday and through baptism?

2. In one parish, children who were not yet receiving eucharist were dismissed following the homily. As they went with their leaders, one little boy stopped the presider, and seem to have a conversation. At the intercessory prayer the presider introduced the prayer and the assembly prayed spontaneously for the needs of the community. When praying for the sick of the parish the presider said, "and for this little boy who asked me to pray for his sick brother." What happens when a community responds to God's word in prayer?

3. John has been with his family at Sunday eucharist since he was a baby. He walks in procession imitating all the postures but, at five, does not yet receive communion. His parents think he's too young. John runs out ahead of his parents crying. He says, "Jesus never turned anyone away from his table, I don't know why Fr. Steve would." Who is ready to participate fully in the eucharist? Who is not? What makes us ready?

4. "Go in peace." Discuss what implications an inclusive celebration has for the life of the community.

CONCLUSION

Towards Practical Decisions

In this book, the task put before you was to look with a critical eye at your Sunday assembly. Children are in our assemblies every Sunday and they come to worship God. These liturgies are not neutral for them. They either affect them positively or negatively. They either build or destroy our children's faith. Our challenge is to prepare for and preside over worship that builds our faith as a community.

Now that you have reflected on your experience of children in the Sunday assembly in light of our tradition, it is time to return to doing, to practice. It is time for practical decisions that will shape next Sunday's gathering of God's people in your community.

Decisions

The work begins here. All of us are affected by what we encounter. Some of your attitudes may have been affirmed or challenged. In any event the action rests with those, like you, who have taken steps to deepen their understanding of what it means to be church. To help make some decisions the following might be useful.

Draw out a picture of the ideal liturgy as you see it ...
This vision suggests changes ...
The assembly needs to ...
The positive aspects already in place are ...
What needs to be overcome is ...
I need conversion in ...
My greatest struggle is ...
My greatest strength is ...
Children are capable of ...
Children need our help in ...

My supports include ...
I imagine in six months ...
I imagine in two months ...
I imagine in three weeks ...
By next season ...
What is the energy level ...
The decisions we are making in our parish are ...

GLOSSARY

Assembly: the local weekly gathering of God's people for praise and worship.

Paschal mystery: the life, death and resurrection of Jesus Christ, the pouring out of the Holy Spirit and our sharing in this mystery through baptism, confirmation and eucharist.

BIBLIOGRAPHY

Recommended Reading

Official Documents

Directory for Masses with Children (1973).

The General Instruction on the Roman Missal (1969)

The Rite of Baptism for Children (1989)

Books

Bernstein, Eleanor, CSJ, and John Brooks-Leonard. *Children in the Assembly of the Church.* Chicago: Liturgy Training Publications, 1992.

Duggan, Robert D. and Maureen Kelly. *The Christian Initiation of Children.* Mahwah, NJ: Paulist Press, 1991.

Halmo, Joan. *Celebrating the Church Year with Young Children.* Ottawa, Novalis: 1988.

Matthews, Edward. *Celebrating Mass with Children.* NY: Paulist Press, 1978.

McMahon Jeep, Elizabeth, et al. *The Welcome Table: Planning Masses with Children.* Chicago: Liturgy Training Publications, 1982.

Miffleton, Jack. *Sunday's Child.* Washington, D.C.: Pastoral Press, 1989.

Ng, David & Virginia Thomas. *Children in the Worshipping Community.* John Knox Press, Atlanta, Georgia, 1981.

Pottebaum, Gerard A., Sister Paule Freebrug, D.C. and Joyce M. Kelleher. *A Child Shall Lead Them.* Loveland, Ohio: Treehaus Communications Inc., 1992.

Periodicals

Paul J. Leblanc, "Directory for Masses with Children: "Purpose" of elements should correspond," *Living Worship 10* (May 1974).

Nathan Mitchell, "The parable of childhood," *Liturgy 1* (June 1981) 7-12.

Nathan Mitchell, "Symbols Are Actions, Not Objects", *Living Worship*, Liturgical Conference, February 1977, vol. 13, no. 2.

Lawrence E. Mick, "Ten Commandments for Presiding at Masses With Children," *Liturgy* 90, May-June 1995.

Linda Gaupin, CDP, "The Liturgical Life of Our Children," *Oregon Catholic Press,*1992.

National Bulletin on Liturgy:

"Children Learn to Celebrate," vol. 16, no. 89, May-June 1983.

"Children and Liturgy," vol. 23, no. 121, June 1990.

"Nonverbal Dimensions of the Eucharist," vol. 22, no. 118, September 1989.

"Helping Families to Pray," vol. 14, no. 80, September-October 1981.